Dedication

To all the innocent casualties of Man's atrocities

Introduction

Dateline: Global Space: 07-01-2022: 12 PM (GMT)

All the elements that gave rise to the World War i (WWI) and World War ii (WWII) are currently at play: expansionism, dictatorship, voluntary and forced alliances, world economic crises, recession, mismanagement of global relationships and of course attack on a sovereign nation!

 Is this 'the day of the jackal' ? Has World War iii pundits day of reckoning come?

Ofcourse, war excites man and that is why men conjure war, why not? Mankind keep advancing, developing and amassing leather weapons, simply because it is conjuring and expecting wars, but everyone comes up with the 'Holy excuse' -to deter war.

Since the end of World War ii, there have been wars: in Africa, in Europe, in Asia and many more isolated conflicts, but it seems what this generation craved most is a war in a global scale, a World war iii and to actualize it, war mongers and world war iii pundits have been pushing the possibilities with conspiracy theories which are appealing, loved, enjoyed and looked forward to by many, especially the gullible because it distracts some of them from some other worries. But the fallacy is that everyone hopes that it will be staged in another person's backyard while they watch on television and follow on social media channels.

Little has majority realised that for every weapon manufactured, someone is looking up for a trade to make a business profit, and for every weapon traded, someone is looking up for opportunities to use it to destroy lives and properties just to justify a cause or the other. This is the primary reason for arms bazaar, the 'Achilles heels' of world peace.

"NOBODY HAS MONOPOLY OF VIOLENCE...IF YOU GIVE IT, THEN BE READY TO TAKE IT"

– REUBEN-LAURENCE NZEWI

"I KNOW NOT WHAT WEAPONS WORLD WAR III WILL BE FOUGHT, BUT WORLD WAR IV WILL BE FOUGHT WITH STICK AND STONES "

–ALBERT EINSTEIN

CHAPTER 1

ANOTHER BAZAAR FOR THE VULTURES

The world is an exciting place because forces of light and darkness are constantly interfacing to keep mankind excited. Perhaps, GOD knows the best, HE could have created a saintly world devoid of any form of evil, yet HE decided to grant the devil his wish to come down to earth to garnish the world with some evil…, yet again, so merciful HE planted in man the holy spirit to give man direction in order not to fall to the manipulations and tricks of the devil; God is indeed very democratic to give man the liberty to choose between light and darkness. But it seems man is constantly and obviously walking his steps to darkness and to that effect produced two devastating world wars in the last century; World War I (1914-1918) and World War II (1939-1945) and seemingly headed to the third-just waiting for the perfect excuse.

*** Europe and its palaver**

WORLD WAR I

The Political instability in the Balkans (South-East Europe), particularly Bosnia, Serbia and Herzegovina was the primary course of the first world war, but it was the murder of Archduke Franz Ferdinand , Heir to the Austro-Hungarian Empire and his wife Sophia in Sarajero, Bosnia by a Serbian nationalist Gavrilo princip on June 28, 1914 that actually sparked the war. Soon after the murder tensions escalated with the super powers and alliances taking sides on the conflict. While Germany, Austria- Hungary, Bulgaria and the Ottoman empire(Turkey) converged under the Central Powers, the Great Britain, France, Russia, Italy, Romania, Canada, converged under the Allied Powers and a 'climate of hell" was unleashed on humanity. And by the time the dust settled with the Allied Powers claiming victory, more than 16 million were dead (a bargain bazaar for the vultures) It should be noted that this war was made possible because humanity have conjured it. It is by conjuring and anticipating wars that humanity keep advancing war technologies and amassing weapons and only looking for an excuse or opportunity to justify one. In the case of World War I the killing of Franz Ferdinard was the perfect excuse and opportunity – Austria-Hungary, like many other countries around the world blamed the Serbian

WORLD WAR II.

Another political instability in Europe, another world War. One of the tenets of World War 1 was to settle the 'Serbian nationalism question' once and for all. And for the world War II one of the tenets in Adolph Hitlers terms was to settle the 'Jewish question' once and for all. 'The Final Solution' he calls it.

Actually, it was the unresolved issues which arose out of World War I that created political and economic instability in Europe, practically in Germany and the Lingering resentment over the harsh terms imposed by the victorious Allied powers as contained in the Versailles Treaty .All these provided a young charismatic Hitler the platform to rise to power through his National Socialist Party, NSDAP otherwise known as the Nazi Party. Coming to his tenet of 'final solution', supremist Hittler had long nursed the devilish intent of exterminating the Jewish race which he gave intent in his memoir 'mein Kempf' as far back as 1923.

As usual, the elements that brews a war started as soon as Hitler took over power. First, he anointed himself as the supreme leader, just as Putin has done in Russia, Xi Jinping in China and Kim Jung-Un in North-Korea. Secondly he started amassing arms against the Versailles Treaty and to perfect his plan, he went ahead to sign alliances with Japan and Italy including signing a non aggression pact with Joseph Stalin, the then leader of the Soviet union. Then on September 1, Hittler invaded Poland and two days later Britain and France declared war on Germany. Yet, another bazaar for the vultures with about 50 million deaths.

Militarism, Alliances, Dictatorship and overzealous nationalism were clearly visible as the building blocks for World War I and World War II. These elements usually arise when big countries with large economy and big armies, especially the ones governed by dictators and overzealous nationalists become potential threat to other countries, which in turn spurs countries with less economic and military endowment to seek protection by way of voluntary or forced alliances to secure their land and sovereignty.

Can mankind ever learn? It seems we are at it again. All the elements for a perfect brew for another World War are playing out in the globe. Today, we have three leaders with enormous resources and military might who are diehard dictators. Namely: Vladimir Putin of Russia, Xi Jinping of China and Kim Jung-Un of North Korea. Secondly, militarism and arms armament are brazenly displayed by some of these leaders and we have seen frenzied alliances in recent times with NATO expanding in all fronts, and in Eastern Europe, Russia is seeing the eastward expansion of NATO as a threat to its national security and an act of provocation. To counter NATO, Russia has inspired the creation of CSTO-collective security treaty organizations, an alliance of 6 former Soviet states.

As of dateline, there is a new one in the pipeline, AUKUS. This is being put together by the United States, the United Kingdom and Australia to secure the pacific in nuclear weapon terms- seen as a measure to counter China in that axis.

Ironically, a world that want peace is developing, advancing and amassing the deadliest weapon unimaginable.

Today the United states and Russia own a 'doomsday' a specialized plane designed as a military control in the air. Military experts claim it can remain airborne for days. It is built in case of a nuclear attack, to enable the operator control its nuclear weapon anywhere in the world. There is also the mushroom cloud nuclear bomber capable of detonating tens of megatons of TNT . There are also chemical and biological weapons of different capabilities, all made with the intent of obliterating humanity.

What more evidence do we need to conclude that humanity is indeed conjuring, abating and anticipating wars? To settle one nagging 'question'; the World War I was to settle the 'Serbian nationalism question', while the World War I was to settle the 'Jewish question'. Is it time to settle the 'Ukraine sovereignty question'?

WORLD WAR III IN PIECEMEAL.

The world war III is already in progress, is it not unfolding before our eyes. The Russian- Ukranian crises may have attracted more media attention and global interests, but suffice to say that the World war III has begun long ago, though fought in a piecemeal. While we have not acknowledged it is that it has not been galvanized and organized into central commands like Allied powers, Central powers or Axis powers like we had in the first and second World Wars. In this particular war by piecemeal, both state actors and non state actors (terrorist groups) are all in it, perpetuating whole sales massacre of people and destruction of properties for one reason or the other: Religious, Cultural, Political or Economic. Already in the melee are: Somalia,

Myanmar, Israel, the US, South Sudan, Afghanistan, Syria, Russia, Ukraine Palestine, Yemen, Saudi Arabia, Nigeria, Hezbollah, Al-Qaeda, Boko-Haram, ISWAP, ISIS, Fulani Herdsmen, Nigeria's banditry and the list goes on.

So , what war mongers and world war III pundits are asking for is the "icing in the cake" (a candidate to give it a global flavor)

"NEVER THINK THAT WAR, NO MATTER HOW NECCESSARY, NOR HOW JUSTIFIED, IS NOT A CRIME"

– ERNEST HEMINGWAY

"OUR NUCLEAR WEAPON IS TO DETER WAR, BUT IF ANY PEOPLE RISES AGAINST NORTH KOREA'S INTERESTS, SUCH PEOPLE WILL STOP TO EXIST "

–KIM JUNG-UN

CHAPTER 2

WORLD WAR III PUNDITS AND THE DRAGON LINES

Modern economics have captured 'varieties ' as one of the primary needs of man. In other words, after food, shelter, clothing and intimacy Man still need to be kept excited and this mankind has provided by various means of entertainment; music, arts and various global sports events like the Olympics and numerous World Cups: football, rugby, basketball, tennis etc, all this to keep humanity excited and entertained. But it seems, the crush of bones & flesh and the smell of blood is what man crave most and so badly, that is why since the turn of the 21st century the world has been looking up for opportunities for world war III. So the world war III pundits and war mongers have been permutating conspiracies that could lead to that, but non yet have materialized. But they have kept hope alive and to make it appealing and marketable to the next generation, they have coined several Fancy words to describe it – Star wars, digital war, cyber war and nukky wars etc.

The pundits closest conspiracies to World war iii includes the USA 9/11 attack, the Syria triangle of evil, the US/Iran faceoff and of course the Corona virus imbroglio. And now Putin's war.

THE US 9/11 ARMAGEDOM

The armagedom that was unleashed on the pride of the United states of America on September 11 2001 was the kind of attack that preludes a mega conflict. Everybody thought that the World war iii that humanity has been conjuring has downed on us.

'' I quickly shower, got dressed, I get into my car and I see a plane flying low over the Potomac . And then I see smoke right where the pentagon is, and I said to myself, Oh my GOD. This is world war III'

– U.S Senate Majority Leader, Charles Schumer.

The world war iii pundits and war mongers had hoped it had been Russia, Iran, North Korea or any of those opposing forces, but at the end of the day, their permutations and conspiracy theory were thrashed; It was a novel attack by a gang of muslim extremist- The al-Qaeda led by a Saudi national, Osama Bn Laden. The group was isolated, pursued and destroyed and their patron, the Taliban government in Afghanistan was toppled. So the 9/11 attack did not produce the 21st century world war- The WWIII

The hijackers in the 9/11 attacks were 19 men affiliated with the extremist Islamic group al-Qaeda. They hailed from four countries. 15 of them were citizens of Saudi Arabia, two were from the United Arab Emirates, one from Lebanon and one from Egypt. During the attacks, 2977 people were killed and more than 6000 were injured. Of the 2977 deaths, 2763 were in the world trade center and the surrounding area, 189 were at the Pentagon and 44 were in Pennsylvania.

THE SYRIA TRIANGLE OF EVIL

Ordinarily the Syrian crisis is an internal affair between the government, the 'rebels' (interim government) and the Islamic State (ISIS). But when the crises came to full bloom, it became a triangular evil of internal and external foes. And when Russia and the US took sides in the conflicts; Russia standing with the government and Political Leadership of Syria and the US with the rebels (Interim Government). Tension become increasingly heightened between Washington and Moscow which gave war mongers and the world war iii pundits a glimmer of hope that an overzealous Russia strike or US Strike could provoke a direct conflict between the two but non has occured, but the pundits and mongers are still hoping.

So far, the alliances and support look as a perfect brew for a Wirld war iii

**For the Syrian Arab Republic (incumbent government)-Hezbollah, Iran, Russia and Egypt.

**For the 'rebels' (Interim government)- U.S.A, Turkey, Quater , U.K, France, Saudi-Arabia.

** For the Free Syrian Army-Jordan, Netherlands, Australia.

**For the Islamic State (IS) – Al-Qaeda and its affiliate groups

THE CORONA VIRUS IMBROGLIO

The Covid-19 Pandemic was another dragon line for the world war iii pundits. This was a novel biological attacks on humanity, by who? Nobody knows. The Virus was discovered in the

Chinese city of Wuham in December of 2019. Soon the conspiracy theories began with Trump's America trying frantically to blame China for the attack. And when China responded appropriately and aggressively the hope of the world war iii pundits were rekindled as they see it as another dimension of the trade war between the US and China and hoped it could degenerate to military confrontation. But at the end they were disappointed as the world came together to fight the virus as a common enemy.

At the break of the pandemic, two conspiracy theories on the origin of the virus emerged. One was pointing accusing fingers at China- According to Dossier uncovered by the US state department some six years ago, China was preparing for a third world war with biological weaponry, including the Corona virus. While the other theory blamed the US. By and large, both theories make claims of biological warfare attempts. Because biological weaponry is increasingly becoming an option for nations, and terrorist groups who are driven by hunger for power and dominion to access and exercise its super destructive potentials.

US/ IRAN FACEOFF

Iran is always a top dog for global conflicts. This has always been there since the moslem extremists over ran the pro-west Shah dynasty in the late 70's and followed it up with the Iraq-Iran War. Iran is always in a dragon line, if it is not Middle-East imbroglio with Israel, It is nuclear weapon development palaver with the US and the rest of the West. One political commentator once put it that Iran farms crisis like the Irish farm potato. So barely 3 days into

2020 an air strike by the U.S army ordered by Donald Trump killed Iranian 2nd in command, Qassim Suleimani, prompting the supreme leader of Iran, Ayatolah Khomeini to warn that the strike will be met by harsh 'consequences ' In return Trump fired back in his usual sarcastic manner that "Iran has never won a war'' .The ensuing tension then gave the World war iii pundits a glimmer of hope again as they drew parallel lines for Donald Trump and Ayatollah Khomeini.

What even inspired the pundits' hope the more is that the killing of Sulemani bears resemblance to the killing of Franz Ferdinand in Sarejeo, Bosnia that culminated into the second world war. This too did not produce the much awaited WWIII as time and events mellowed tensions. But war mongers and world war iii pundits have not lost hope yet.

The Shah Dynasty

Iran was ruled by the Pro-West Shah Mohammed Reza Pahlavi before he was over thrown by Ayatollah Ruhollah Khomeini and his Islamic Revolutionalist in 1979 to establish the Iran Islamic Republic.

Iraq-Iran War

In September 1980, Iraqi forces under the command of president Saddam Hussein launched a full scale invasion of Iran fueled by territorial, religious, economic and political disputes between the two countries, particularly the control of the shatt al-arab, the water way formed by the confluence of the Tigris and Euphrates Rivers. After 8 years, the conflict ended in a stalemate and a ceasefire with about half a million deaths of soldiers and civilians alike

"IF MANKIND WANT TO STOP WARS, THEN EVERYDAY PEOPLE OF THE WORLD MUST RISE UP AGAINST DICTATORSHIP, OVERZEALOUS NATIONALISTS, EXPANSIONISM, MILITARISM AND FRENZIED ALLIANCES"

~ REUBEN-LAURENCE NZEWI.

"ONLY THE DEAD HAVE SEEN THE END OF WAR"

~ GEORGE SANTAYANA.

CHAPTER 3

THE WORLD MOST DANGEROUS MAN

Since the world crave for world war iii, a candidate is needed to instigate it- "the anointed one". So since the turn of the century the world war iii pundits have been drawing up a short list of possible candidates. The candidates are men with the capability to provoke major global crises based on the political, economic and military capabilities of the country they lead, and of course their behavioral pattern. And in the last few years four presidents have featured in that list namely:: Vladamir Putin of Russia, Donald Trump of the U.S.A, Xi Jinping of China and Kim Jung-un of North Korea.

Vladamr Putin:

Mean, cold and calculating. Mr. Putin made the pundits list of the world most dangerous man on the basis of his behavioral pattern and the country he leads (Russia)

Russia's Soviet union was established in 1920 after the Russian Revolution in 1917 and the subsequent 3 years civil war under the leadership of Vladimir Lenin and his Bolshevik party. The Bolshevik regime dominated Soviet Union and grew into one of the world most powerful and influential nations and the first country in the world to be based on Marxist socialism, and emerged as the alternate world power at the end of world War II.

With a distinct economic ideology of communion and fifteen republics folded into the Soviet Union under the headship of Russia; Russia's Soviet Union possesed the land mass, natural and human resources and military capability to checkmate any contrary force to its interests. In 1991 the almighty Soviet Union crumbled giving rise to 15 independent republics of

Russia, Ukraine, Belarus, Georgia, Uzbeikitan, Armenia, Azerbaijan kazakstan, Kyrgyzstan, Moldova, Turkmenistan, Tajkistan, Latvia, Lithuania and Estonia. Yet, after the Soviet union disintegration, Russia on itself still emerged as the force it was, even more prosperous engendered by enormous natural resources and more robust economic system, now under the leadership of charismatic, but cold and calculating Mr. Vladamir Putin.

On the back drop of a secret intelligence background and former head of the KGB (FSB) – one of the world's most efficient secret service, Mr Putin is not a man to toy with. He has a meaness that is eerie, and always 'cold' and 'calculating'.

From KGB chief to Prime Minister under Boris Yeltsins administration, Mr. Putin became president after Mr. yelsin dramatically resigned as the president of Russia. Since Mr. Putin became president, he has bolstered Russia's standing in the global community; Russia is respected and revered under Putin. He has also gotten Russia involved in major conflicts both within and outside, he annexed Crimea in 2014 to ward off Ukraine. He also got Russia fully involved in the Syria triangle of evil, supporting the government of Syria under Bashar al-Assad with air strikes against the rebels (Interim government forces) and ISIS gangs.

But what really put Putin as a top candidate for world most dangerous man is his new found statue – Mr. Putin is a super dictator and an overzealous nationalist (twin elements that always brew global conflict). Mr. Putin has sublimed Russia's political and democratic space to gain absolute power since he took over from Boris Yelsin on December 1999. Putin has also set a stage as one of the most powerful leaders of Russia after Peter De Great. He has embezzled enormous political, social and financial powers for him to remain invincible, not only in Russia but in Europe and at the global stage, and above all these Mr. Putin possesses spiritual powers ordained by 'chernobog' the Slavic god of bad fate and chaos. There was a scoop some years back that Vladamir Putin's favorite song is 'Ras-putin' a 1978 hit track from the band group

'Bonny M'. It is believed that Vladamir Putin shares similar fate with Grigori Ras Putin from 'chernobog'. And he is World war iii pundits favorite candidate to instigate their much awaited World war iii.

Grigory Rasputin was a mythic figure in 20th century Russia in the court of Czar Nicholas ii of Russia. He plays the role of mystical advisor to Czar Nicholas II. He was alleged to be possessed by 'chernobog' and have hypnotic powers over the king and his household. Mr. Rasputin was revered and at the same time loathed for being a sex-crazed maniac who was having a secret affair with the queen. In the early morning of December 29 1916 Grigory Rasputin was murdered by Russian nobles eager to end his influence over the Royal Family. That was how the life and time of Grigory Rasputin was ordained, programmed and destroyed by 'chernobog' ,the Slavic god of bad fate.

Kim Jung-Un:

He is young, mean, ruthless and loves nukes. His name is Kim Jung Un. He is North Korea's supreme leader since 2011. The North Korea's strong man makes the shortlist of the pundits world's most dangarous man. It is alleged that Kim Jung-un's favourite past time (hobby) is testing nukes, the 'boy' loves developing and testing nukes. Close watchers say he normally visits his country's nuclear weapon projects sites to 'caress' the deadly devices and often likened them to his ultimate 'joker'. While the Corona virus threat curve was spiking in his country , Kim still find time to test his nukes and according to him the event was meant to 'llighten-up' the mood of his country men who were depressed by the pandemic. Kim Jung-un and his North Korea power drunk gang want global power at all cost. Kim and his men are waiting for the perfect excuse to show the world what they are up to, but the world does not feel comfortable with Kim and his ' holy satans' in Possession of nuclear weapon. So the world war iii pundits and war mongers are eagerly waiting for the 'flash point' and that is what is giving them a glimmner of hope that the 'mad man' in North Korea could realize for them the much awaited World war iii.

Character wise, kim is ruthless, he has tested blood and can do with some more.

Kim is the son of Kim Jong-il who was North Korea's second supreme leader from 1994 to 2011.

He is a grandson of Kim Il-Sung, who was the founder and first supreme leader of North Korea since it was established in 1948 until his death in 1994.

Now that Kim Jung-Un is in the saddle, he has turned into a notorious dictator and appropriated all political powers through a constitution which gives his political party (The Workers Party) supremacy over other parties. It is alleged that he ordered the murder of his half brother Kim Jong – nam in Malasia in 2017. And also ordered the execution of his uncle Jang song Thaek two years after succeeding his father. As a deterrent, Jang Song Thaek headless body, with the head sitted on the chest of the lifeless body was displayed to the senior government officials.

So far as Kim Jung-un is around, the world has plenty to worry about as he has this to say at the 90th anniversary of North Korea's Army Foundation. Kim said that his nuclear weapon is to "deter war" but if any contrary force tries to undermine North Korea, such people will stop to 'exist'.

Donald Trump

This man is known to be flamboyant, vociferous and controversial. At the beginning of the Russia – Ukraine conflicts, he hailed Putin as 'smart' and 'genius' but when the condemnation of Putin actions started gaining momentum he changed stance and in one statement he said "if I were in power I would have bombed the shit out of Russia". That is Donald Trump for you. Now you know why he makes world war iii pundit's top candidate to provoke world war iii.

Before he became the president of the United States of America, Mr. Trump was a very colorful character and very entrepreneurial. He was a real estate mogul, a very creative mind, being the founder of the Miss world beauty pageant and yet, a great TV personality as the founder of the box office reality TV show, ' The apprentice' . As the helsman of the richest and strongest nation in the world, in addition to his behavioral pattern and tendency of overzealous nationalism, Mr. Trump made it as a potential provocateur of world war iii. Little wonder, a commentator once put it that if Trump weakens the US commitment to NATO (which he hinted) he will surpass Putin as the world most dangerous man.

Trump has once talked about responding to terrorist attacks with nuclear weapon and reflecting on what he would have done if he were still the president of the United States in the face of Russia's invasion of Ukraine, Mr. Trump said "I would say we have far more nuclear weapons than you do, far more powerful than you and you can't use that word 'nuclear weapon ever again. And if you do, we're going to have problem and Russia would no longer exist should the US deploy it's own arsenal". In 2017, Donald Trump also prompted the Bulletin of the Atomic Scientists, operators of the 'Doomsday clock ' to move it 30 seconds closer midnight. The symbolic moment mankind is supposed to annihilate itself. Trumps inspired movement of the clock was the closest mankind have come to the brink since 1953 when the first hydrogen bomb was launched. The doomsday clock operators cited Trump's statement about the use of nuclear weapons, as he tweeted in December 2016 that " the United States must greatly strengthen and expand its nuclear capability until such a time as the world comes to its senses regarding nukes". This is how much Donald Trump is perceived to be dangerous.

Since the war in Ukraine started, Mr. Trump has been making sarcastic comments which are true to his character, maybe the 'gods' are wise to take him out of power before Putin's madness started. Though he made the pundit's list, Mr. Trump is now harmless. He can only bark now, sure he has no fangs to bite.

XI Jinping

He is cool, calm and gentlemanlike. Xi Jinping eminently makes the world war iii pundit's list of world's most dangerous man. Jinping's calm demeanor does not reveal his intensity and ruthlessness. Since he came to power on 14th March, 2014. Jinping has systematically gained absolute power in China, a feat the much revered Chairman Mao did not even achieve. He has eliminated or sidelined political competitors and crafted a one-man personality clout never seen in China. And by scrapping term limit in the country's constitution, Jinping has awarded himself the right to rule for life. Jinping's clout comes mainly from the fact that China today is the second largest economy in the world, and its rise to that enviable position gives him the leeway that non of his predecessors had. More so, China's rise as world economic power has come on the back of a high degree of integration with the global economic grid, that only adds to its clout as it is economically indispensable for now; China manufactures more than 20% of world trade- UNCTAD

With his absolute power statue and China's new found 'enormous' resource, the world will be in trouble if expansionism and leather weaponry fascinates Xi Jimping the more.

In restrospect, the China that Xi Jinping leads today is a very different one from China of the 90's when leaders in the West hoped Beijing could be teased into opening up and integrating China smoothly and democratically into the global order created by the West, but the body language shows that Xi Jinping has other plans. He is evolving China into a super power capable of throwing it's weight around the world stage in its own order.

Chairman Mao:

Chairman Mao Zedong was the founder of the Peoples Republic of China (PRC) on the 1st of October, 1949 with communist ideology after several wars and victories notable the defeat of Chiang Kai-shek of the KMI warring group, an erstwhile ally who fled to the Island of Taiwan to found his own 'independent' state.

"THOSE WHO WANT TO LIVE, LET THEM FIGHT, AND THOSE WHO DO NOT WANT TO FIGHT IN THIS WORLD OF ETERNAL STRUGGLE DO NOT DESERVE TO LIVE "

~ ADOLF HITLER.

Chapter 4

CHERNOBOG

Remember Judas Iscariot; the most infamous character in the holy bible, he is one of the twelve disciples of Jesus Christ, he is also the treasurer of the group, and the one who betrayed Jesus Christ by collecting money to point him out to the enemies.

Poor Judas, programmed and destroyed by the gods...sorry God. Villains are chosen and programmed by the gods to achieve a devilish purpose before they are destroyed. That was the fate of Adolph Hilter too and other infamous characters in recent history: Benito Mussolini of Italy, saddam Hussein, Osama Bin Laden e.t.c. The devil and his band of demons do not have physical energy, so for them to unleash their terror, their lease a human carrier....that is it, and just like God manifests Himself in man as holy spirit to do good, so does Satan manifest itself in man as demonic spirits to cause havoc

 CHERNOBOG is the Slavic god of bad fate and chaos. Also known as the black god in Slavic mythology. A myth had it that at the age of 12 Vladamir Putin was said to have passed into coma "trance" during which he communed with CHERNOBOG who promised to make him the most feared man in Europe.

 It was in 1923, that Adolf Hilter aged 34 predicted the Second World War in his infamous memoir 'Mein Kempf' (my Struggles). But the world never knew that Hilter was possessed by TYR, the German God of war. Hilter encountered TYR when he fainted from gas poisoning inside a trench in the heat of the First World War. Possessed by TYR and obsessed by wars, Hitler premeditated the Second World War after testing blood in the first war which he himself miraculously survived with 15 million deaths. Aided by the gods, Hilter manipulated the democratic and political structures to gain power and assume the supreme leader and a notorious dietator before he began the rearmament of the German army. Then he went on to forge evil alliances particular with Japan and Italy, and followed it up with nonaggression pact with the Soviet Union under Joseph Stalin, before unleashing his terror with the attack on Austria and the Czechoslovakia. Just like Hilter, Mr Putin premeditated his war on Ukraine and maybe much more. He has studiously followed the Hilter template. Dramatically Boris Yelsin resigned and power fell to him. He has intimidated and manipulated the political landscape in Russia to attain absolute power and started the massive military buid up, unmatched in human history with an annual military budget of $42b, 3.5m personnel reserve, 13,000 tanks, 27000 amoured vehicle, 4465 artillery guns, 6257 nuclear war heads and much more.

While the world is worrying its heads on what putin will do or not do, Putin possessed by the gods premeditated his war and knows where he is going and what he want to achieve. Putin is obsessed to be feared by Europe such that when he sneezes, Europe will catch cold. That is what he wants and the gods will grant him his wishes on the condition that he makes a wholesale of human sacrifice. So Ukraine is an unfortunate victim of something they don't know about, even ordinary Russians too who will be at the receiving end of Putin's actions. It was noted that it was after the "trance" and encounter with CHERNOBOG that Putin got fascinated with spy books. He has had it at the back of his mind that someday he will conquer nations and this was what influenced his choice of career and he made good of it by rising through the ranks to become the KGB chief. The gods have been aiding him and waiting and the time has come for him to make returns. Only time will tell whether Mr. putin will swallow the world to fulfill the prophesy of

Baba Vanga 'Nostradamous of the Balkans' , the blind Bulgarian psychic, who in the 70's foretold that Vladamir will rule the world one day. According to reports by Writer Valentin Sidorov (Daily Mail, UK) she said that Russia would become "lord of the world " after Europe become a wasteland. And she continued "all will thaw, as if ice, only one remained untouched; Vladamir, glory, glory of Russia " .

Is Putin the chosen one to actualize World war iii for war mongers and the World war iii pundits? Or will the world vanquish Mr. Putin and his gods?

"TWO ARMIES THAT FIGHT EACH OTHER IS LIKE ONE LARGE ARMY THAT COMMITS SUICIDE"

~ HENRI BARBUSSE.

CHAPTER 5

"THE OTHER ENEMY HELD ALOFT A CROSS"

Men always pretend they can do all things but when vulnerable they rush to hold the Cross (the Cross is actually a symbol of innocence & holiness in christiandom). Who is with the cross, Putin or Zelensky?

The Easter Mass of 17th April in the middle of the crises presented a unique opportunity for both leaders to commune with God for victory over the enemy . while Zelensky was at the Saint Sophia Cathedral in Kiev to seek the face of God… unjustifying Putin's action to invade his country, Zelensky likened the Easter as a great hope for his country as it was a great hope for humanity as Jesus arose from death – in his prayers, Zelensky prayed God to give him victory over his enemy. He said Ukraine has not invaded any country, grabbed any territory of another country by force and that Ukraine has not enslave the citizens of any country, neither has Ukraine killed innocent children, rape innocent women and destroyed properties of innocent people. He also prayed God to return happiness to children and bless and protect those who are supporting Ukraine in the face of Putin's invasion. Across the border just 230 miles from Kiev, putin was at the Christ The Savior Cathedral in Moscow, where he justified his action before God.. In the same vein, he asked God for victory over his enemy as he claimed to God that he (Putin) is the one holding the cross with strong support from Kirill, the patriarch of Moscow and the primate of Russian orthodox church who claimed God is on Russian side and likened the war to a "holy war". Meanwhile, the Pope in Rome, Pope Francis has warned Kirill to stop being putin's 'barkdog'. The Pope thinks Mr. Putin is on a mission to test his powers and prove something to Europe and the world, and Ukraine is the unfurtunate gumea pig for that experiment. Poor Ukraine, you must hold on to the Cross. Though every one claims to be holding the Cross. Only the Cross knows who is holding it, only time shall tell.

Ukraine is a moderate populated country with moderate economic endowment. The 2nd most populated East Slavic nation after Russia, with a population of 43,243,351 people. The Russia-Ukraine crises began immediately after the Soviet Union's disintegration, because of the two compelling forces in the Ukrainian body politics. Those that want to maintain the Pro-Russia political alignment and the Pro-West forces that want to keep farther away from Russia with preference to embrace the West. Ordinarily, the everyday people of Russia and Ukraine do not want war because they are fraternized for a very long time. Russians and Ukrainians are cousins to each other.

"IF CHANGE HAS NOT COME, IT MEANS THE WILL OF THEM THAT WANT THINGS TO REMAIN SAME IS STRONGER THAN THE WILL OF THOSE THAT WANT CHANGE "

-REUBEN-LAURENCE NZEWI

CHAPTER 6

DELUDED WORLD

Hostillities between Russia and Ukraine actually started in 2014 when Russia annexed Crimea, and Russia backed separatist seize parts of the south-eastern Region of Ukraine. Russia accused Ukraine of being governed by Neo-Nazis who persecute the ethnic Russia minority. Putin also fingersd the North Atlantic Treaty Organization (NATO) as constituting a threat to Russia national security by expanding east-ward and bar Ukraine from ever joining the organization permanently. On the 21st February, 2022, Russia recognized the Donesk peoples republic and the Luhansk peoples republic, two self-proclaimed statelets in Donbas controlled by pro-Russia separatists. The invasion began on 24th February, 2022 when putin announced a "special" military operation to 'demilitarize' and 'denazify" Ukraine and followed it up with missile and air strikes across Ukraine. In response, Ukraine president Volodomyr Zelensky enacted martial law and general mobilization of all male Ukraine citizens for between the ages of 18 and 60, who were barred from leaving the country. As expected the international community rose and widely condemned the invasion as an act of aggression. The United Nation General Assembly adopted a resolution which demanded a full withdrawal of Russia forces. While the international court of justice ordered Russia to suspend operations.

SMART AMERICA

But amidst all the rantings, political and diplomatic statements all eyes were on the United States of America; the aclaimed 'police' of the world. The world was waiting for the reaction and response of America, even though the attack was not on America or America's interest. The world war iii pundits and war mongers were praying America gets directly involved, to realize they dream of 21st Century world war. Indeed, America reacted by condemning the attack on Ukraine sovereignty like the rest of the free world ... But America needed much more wisdom to respond. Ukraine is under attack and she looks up to America for help, and as the big- brother, America has to come to their rescue. Zelensky was under siege by a mighty force, and in specific term he wanted America to join the frail.... then America responded with the objective not to expand the perimeters of the conflicts and escalate the consequences. 'Smart' America opted for elaborate sanctions and military aids. By so doing, America has bought time to reduce the tempo of the conflicts and avoid direct confrontation with Russia. Smart America reasoned that the best option is to continually weaken Russia through continuous military aids to Ukraine, backed with heary sanction from America and NATO allies. Alas, a deluded world that is blood thirsty was disappointed; America is smarter.

SMART NATO

 NATO's Europe eastwards expansion was one of Putin's grouse against Ukraine which makes NATO a party to the conflict. Now, Zelensky was cornered and desperate ... ,but he must survive Putin's onslaught ..., so, he played a fast one by asking NATO to declare Ukraine a no-fly zone for Russia planes….. If NATO obliged Zelensky, it means NATO will shoot down any Russian plane in Ukraine air space ... which will ultimately expand the perimeter of the conflicts and bring Russia, USA and NATO into direct confrontation but NATO was smarter to decline Zelensky request, while working on other means of weakening Russia without direct involvement and confrontation. This too is another huge disappointment for war mongers and the world war iii pundits.

"POWER TENDS TO CORRUPTS, AND ABSOLUTE POWER CORRUPTS ABSOLUTELY "

– LORD ACTON

CHAPTER 7

POLICING THE WORLD: Russia's "Achilles heels"

Hitherto, Russia has allowed and perpetuated a leadership that is a threat to Russia's future for allowing individuals to hijack state powers for their personal ego massage and that is not far fetched from Putin's penchant for brandishing nuclear weapon threats to the world. According to Boris Johnson (British Prime Minister), in an interview in Madrid during NATO meeting in July of 2022, Vladimir Putin has threatened nuclear attacks dozens of times. Johnson pointed out that analysis found 'about 35 mentions by Putin. Mr. Putin is simply telling the world that anybody that provokes his anger in the conflicts with Ukraine will get a dose of his nukes, be it the US, EU, NATO, G7, or any sympathizer to Ukraine. Russia's nuclear threats has degenarated so badly that even non military actors in Russia now have the audacity to issue threats to sovereign nations. Dmitry Kisseycov was one of such, a Kremlim allied TV host who once threatened that "'just one launch, Boris Johnson and England is gone once and for all, why play with us" he said. He was actually talking of a simulated nuclear attack off the coast of Donegal that could turn the entire UK and Ireland into a radioactive desert. Russians must sacrifice the head of Putin to appease the world. They must do this to avoid a long term backlash of anything Russian and they must also do this to reclaim their country from power drunk individuals. The good loving people of Russia must show the world that they are a civilized generation, whose judgment and actions are in tandem with modern civility and must come to the truce that a dictatorial and authoritarian leadership is retrogressive to human progress and Russia's survival in particular.

Russia must also purge itself of it seemingly 'inferiority' complex to the West: Russia conglomerated some nations of Eastern Europe to form the Soviet Union in 1920 in order to counter any other forces on earth, Russia also came up with an alternative economic system of communism (a state command economic model), which was to achieve the type of economic acceleration and stability the West achieved with capitalism. But at the end the Soviet union was choked because both the political and economic structures were shrouded in dark. 'Goodman' Mikhail Gobachev came to the rescue with a reform of perestroika & glasnots (restructuring & openness). It did not achieve its full potential but paved the way for a new Soviet union, later Russia.

Introspectively, if Russia must provide the alternative leadership that is desirous of and worthy of emulation, then Russia must purge itself of dictators and overzealous nationalists, now and in the future, because when such individuals become more powerful than state structures and institutions, it will only spell gloomy future for that nation. This is the fate of Russia.

Russia has made tremendous progress since it abandoned the Soviet Union structure and 'state command' economy to embrace liberal economy to some extent. So the truth remains that ordinary Russians want to be part of the liberal world but Russia's self-serving leaders preferred a "caged" generation to achieve personal gains and this is perhaps Boris Bondarev's grouse with Russia's leadership that prompted his resignation from the government as chancellor of the permanent mission of Russian federation to the United Nations.

Moving forward, if Russia want to claim its rightful place in the committee of nations and provide constructive policing of the world, then she must fashion out a national order and foreign policies that will appeal and influence other nations to embrace its leadership. Also, if Russia is keen in providing a vibrant and constructive leadership to the world, then Russia must clean up;

it can not achieve that level of global leadership on a retrogressive democratic model that promote dictatorship, authoritarian and sit-tight despot. Again and again, Russians must understand that it is great institutions that berth great nations and not the other way round. Therefore a great leader is one that builds great institutions that berths a great nation. This is the least the Russian people expect from putin: build for us great state institutions and leave.

It is no gain saying that Putin has so battered the image of Russia that even in the nearest future, no nation would want to get into alliance with it and the actions of otherwise neutral Nordic nations of Sweden and Finland to join NATO in the face of Ukraine invasion is a pointer to that.

"DON'T START A GAME WITH AN ENEMY WHO HAS SUPERIOR KNOWLEDGE AND TACTICS "

— REUBEN-LAURENCE NZEWI.

CHAPTER 8

CHINA'S "SNAKE IN THE MONKEY SHADOW GAME "

It is two decade now since China hit the global economic space with a bang. Since joining the World Trade Organization (WTO) on 1st December 2001, to compete in the liberal global economic space China has stunned and dwarfed many economies. China has bittersweet taste to many economies. China has overtaken many formidable economies within a short period of time and now sits second behind the United State of America with potentials to overtake in the nearest future. Before now the West seems relaxed and pleased with China's direction of progress, with hope she will embrace the West ideas and join the popular 'order' created by the West. But all changed when Xi Jinping started singing a new song. Xi jinping is gradually fashioning a new national order that will position China to throw its weight around the world in its own way which is likely not to appeal to the West. The game is that China is fashioning its own power bloc, an alternative power to the US, EU, NATO and the rest of the West as well as an alternative power to Russia. Now, with the Russia- Ukraine war in progress many eyes are on China to react and respond to the crises (a seemingly "snake in the monkey shadow" game). Conspiracy theorists think it is a good time for China to decide and establish itself as an independent force to reckon with.

Just like Adolph Hitler and Benito Mussolini, Putin needs a side kick and a strong ally to take on the rest of the world. And just like Hitler and Mussolini who attained absolute power through Nascism and fascism as the common ground for their alliance. Putin and Xi Jinping are already on that course. Putin has perpetuated himself as absolute power since he became the president after Bons Yelsin's dramatic resignation. Jinping too has meticulously and suspiciously perpetuated himself in power which makes them birds of same feather. More so, that China and Russia currently enjoy the best relationship they have had since the late 50's. Although they have no formal alliance, the two coutinues to have informal agreements to coordinate diplomatic and economic moves and build up alliance against the United States of America. Now, the world is waiting to see how they will gravitate to that partnership. But China is cautiously watching it's steps, trying to maintain neutral ground and mutual relationships with Russia, Ukraine and the US. Still, conspiracy theorists believe that along the line China will find ways to help Russia without annoying the US, EU and NATO allies, specifically to reduce the effects of the sanctions by the West and NATO allies; let's watch and see. But what if the US and NATO got itself into direct combat with Russia, will China join the free fight on the side of Russia?. As the "snake in the monkey shadow" game is on, China is watching and calculating the US, EU and NATO. At the same time the US, EU and NATO are watching and calculating the steps of China.

Though China's clout comes from its indispensibility in the global trade chain and that is her 'weakest link'. The question is , if China dares the West by aligning with Russia, can it withstand the avalanche of sanctions to her nascent economic growth?

The "snake in the monkey shadow" game is also taking new dimension in form of renewed biological weapon capability. China's nuclear weapon capability may not measure up to the US and Russia, but China's frenzied activities in biological weaponry advancement is a clear indication of where China is headed. She simply want to have an edge in the biological weaponry; giving credence that the Corona virus may have leaked from one of her laboratories.

"IF RUSSIA FIRES ITS NUCLEAR WEAPONS, THERE WILL BE NO RUSSIA ANYMORE. WE HAVE FAR MORE NUCLEAR " THAN THEY HAVE "

~ DONALD TRUMP

CHAPTER 9

PUTIN AND THE SWORD OF DAMOCLES

What will define Putin's success in the Ukrain invasion? Simple, chasing out Zelensky and his government away and installing a pro-Russia puppet government, and achieving independence for the Donesky and Luhansky people. If Mr. Putin achieves this, his invincibility will increase; he will tightened his grip better on Russia and the Pro-West in the region. And the Eastern-gang up will be more respectful, while the US, EU and NATO will lick their wounds and wait for another opportufnity for a payback …. But then it is seen as a defeat to the US, NATO and the rest of the West. But if Putin fails to overun Kiev and also fails to dethrone Zelensky..., even if he succeeds in taking over the Donbass region....it will still seem to be that he is a loser; Zelensky will be emboldened and can go ahead to join the NATO alliance, and if NATO allows it, then Russia is left open by NATO proximity. If this scenario plays out then Putin is caged, the enemies within (the opposition) and the Russian people will gain traction and they will definitely take him down.

 *** Putin's sword of democles*

THE WHIFF OF MONEY:

Putin's alleged secret wealth stash propaganda has surfaced since the war with Ukraine began, likely the handiwork of the opposition or the West. If putin fails in his Ukraine invasion, he would have exposed himself, and the propaganda on his secret wealth stash will gain momentum which will be one of the many excuses to do away with him, his dictatorial tendencies and his gang of looters in Russia's kleptomaniac government who may have looted the treasury the much as Mr. Putin have looted.

The opposition in Russia claims that Putin's legacy of corruption is enormous. The sprawling billion dollar palace sitting on a 190,000 square feet mega mansion dubbed Putin's palace is one of such. According to the opposition his method is to allow the Oligarchs to flourish in Russia's notoriously corrupt economy so long as they share the loot with him.

Putin is alleged to be the world's richest man with palaces, super yatchs and swiss accounts. Even Elon Musk of Tesla, the world's current Richest man believes Mr Putin is Richer than him. Mr. Putin's wealth is estimated to be in the neighbourhood of $2oo billion and above. On paper, Putin eans a paltry $140,000/ annum and has an 800 square foot apartment, a trailer and three cars. But whistle blowers have put up figures to show that Putin is indeed stupendiously rich. They alleged he has the most expensive collection of watches which includes a patek philipper perpetual calendar watch worth $60,000 and a $500,000 A. lange & sohne Turbograph. Putin is also rumoured to be the owner of a beautiful 190,000 square foot mansion sitting atop a cliff that overlooks the black sea. According to reports the money for this extravagant project was laundered through the Russia's 1.3 trillion ruble national project called "Health" in which the state bought expensive medical equipments from a company owned by Putins friends Gorelov and shamalov at a much higher rate than the market price. Putin also owns 19 other mega mansions, 700 cars and a collection of 58 aircrafts and helicopters among them a $716 million dollar plane called "the flying Kremlim" and a $100m mega yatch.

According to Bill Browder in a testimony to the US Senate Judiciary Committee in 2017, Putin amassed most of his wealth after a Moscow court jailed 'Oligarch' Mikhail khodorkovsky in 2003 for fraud and tax evasion. After khodorkovsky's conviction, the other oligarchs went to

Putin and asked him what they needed to do to avoid khodorkovsjy's fate. From what followed it appeared putin's answer was 50%. He wasn't saying 50% for the Russian government or the presidential administration of Russia, but 50% for Vladimir Putin personally. But of course, Putin admitted to a phylosophical wealth. "I am the wealthiest man, not just in Europe but in the whole world: I collect emotions. I am wealthy in that the people of Russia have twice entrusted me with the leadership of a great nation such as Russia, I believe that is my greatest wealth".

No doubt Mr. Putin brought stability and rapid economic growth to Russia. In his first two terms as president he made liberal economic reforms such as the flat income rate of 13% reduced profit tax which reduced the poverty rate in Russia by half and the GDP has grown rapidly since then. But all these achievements will soon be overshadowed by the alleged massive corruption in Russia economy. In 2021 Russia was the lowest rated economy in Europe, standing at an embarrassing 136th of transparency international corruption perception. This is one of Putin's many sword of democles

'DEPUTINIZATION' OF EUROPE – THE EASTERN GANG-UP

The whole world, especially Russia's eastern neighbours have seen what Putin can do if provoked; he can attack at the whimpest excuse and he can use his almighty gas and oil resources as a weapon and he can brandish his nukes. So far as Putin remains the absolute power in Russia his eastern neighbors and the rest of Europe will never be comfortable. This means Mr. Putin has unwittingly set a stage for the emergence of the Eastern-gang up, who will more than before be ready for his excesses. In the war with Ukraine, Putin has thrown up his cards and these are the areas the Eastern-gang up will concentrate on. They have seen his attacking methods which relies on heavy artillery and missiles strikes above this, the war have exposed his supply lines; now they will be proactive on how to checkmate and undermine these attacking methods and supply lines. Mr. Putin's action in Ukraine has also given his Eastern neighbors the reasons to join or form alliances to counter his aggression in the East. Those that are already in NATO will now justify their decision and even encourage others to come on board. Moreover, Putin using his gas resources as a war weapon is the biggest threat to the economy of his Eastern neighbors and Europe at large, who rely heavily on Russian supply line: Hungary 25%, Germany 14%, Ukraine 11%, Poland... Bulgaria and many others. They will work to neutralize it and the US and EU will be more than willing to assist. Also, brandishing his nuclear capabilities at the whimpest excuse is something his eastern neighbors can not live with. This nuclear threats will definitely inspire some nations in the region to start their nuclear armament and I think the US, EU and NATO will encourage such moves to keep Putin and his future Russia at bay. All in all, Mr. Putin has instigated his Eastern neighbors to gang up against Russia now and in the future.

Instead of scaring Russia's neighbors into submission, Putin has ended up driven them to seek shelter under NATO; Russia's number one nemesis, a lesson for Putin and like minds that threat obviously do not turn difficult neighbors into friends. At the end of this imbroglio, Russia's 'threat curve' to Europe will either spike or flattened depending on the outcome of the Ukrainian crisis.

Beyond Putin, Russia will always remain a threat to his eastern neighbors because the precedent of dictatorial leadership have been set, meaning that after Putin power might still fall to one of his lieutenants, a group that has embezzled enormous political, social and financial powers just like Mr. Putin. The Eastern gang-up is another sword of democles that Mr. Putin will have to contend with.

This is what Emmanuel Macron, president of France says to this effect "I think he (Putin) has isolated himself. Isolating oneself is one thing, but being able to get out of it is a difficult path"

"I think and I told him that he is making a historic and fundamental mistake for his people, for himself and for history"

PUTIN AND THE OLIGARCHS: Playing the 'Russian Roulette'

How much has Putin's action hurt the Oligarchs, and how would they react in the long run? If Putin is unable to end his war in a short while and claim victory, the war will drag on and give the Ukrainians more leverage. This will also make the sanctions very effective and gradually the pains and loses will start manifesting in real terms which will ultimately pitch the Oligarchs against Putin. The Oligarchs may be emboldened and start favoring a regime change to minimize their loses. That means the 'unholy' alliance between Mr. Putin and the Oligarchs, which the opposition sees as the root of Russia's notorious corrupt economy will be tested. Will these oligarchs continue to abide and 'flow' with Putin in the face of total damage to their business? Will the two stick together in good and bad times? Putin knows that the only people that have the capacity to ferment trouble for him within are the Olligarchs. They have the capacity to sponsor resentment and protest against him. They also have the capacity to create a fifth culumn in his government and fight him within the inner circle. Putin himself will not like to fallout with his 'holy satans' at this critical times, he would do everything to maintain their relationship. Sure, he would not like to engage the Oligarchs in a game of the 'Russian Roulette'. playing the 'Russian Roulette' with the Oligarchs is yet another sword of democles Mr. Putin will contend with.

The Oligarchs emerged in Russia with the emergence of the new Russia after the disintegration of the Soviet Union. The opportunities created by Russia's economic transition and privatization saw their emergence as Russia's elite money-bags and inner circle government brokers and influencers. But unknown to them, mean and calculating Vladamir Putin was not too comfortable with their expanding influence and when he strucked with the arrest and conviction of Mikhail Khodorkovsky, the wealhiest of the Olligarchs in 2003 the game changed, a perfect strike and the Oligarchs were caged. Gradually their influenced waned and their freedom and wealth were at the mercy of Mr.Putin . In other to reduce the effect of Putin's powers on their wealth they started investing off shore. The move was a smart one, but for the war in Ukraine. Now the intensity and dragnet of the US, EU and NATO sanctions on their wealth abroad is a nightmare that they never anticipated. Their wealth is been reduced to nothingness and their life style badly affected. If they lean towards Putin the US and EU will squeeze harder, if they lean towards the West, Mr. Putin will pull the trigger at them. The question then is how long can the Oligarchs bear the consequences of Putin's war on their personal wealth at home and abroad. The primary objective of the sanctions is to squeeze Russia's wealthiest citizens to pressurize and compel them to put pressure on Putin to end his war in Ukraine. Then the other question is: can these people find any space to restrain Putin now that Putin has reduced their power and

The Oligarchs emerged in Russia with the emergence of the new Russia after the disintegration of the Soviet Union. The opportunities created by Russia's economic transition and privatization saw their emergence as Russia's elite money-bags and inner circle government brokers and influencers. But unknown to them, mean and calculating Vladamir Putin was not too comfortable with their expanding influence and when he strucked with the arrest and conviction of Mikhail Khodorkovsky, the wealhiest of the Olligarchs in 2003 the game changed, a perfect strike and the Oligarchs were caged. Gradually their influenced waned and their freedom and wealth were at the mercy of Mr.Putin . In other to reduce the effect of Putin's powers on their wealth they started investing off shore. The move was a smart one, but for the war in Ukraine. Now the intensity and dragnet of the US, EU and NATO sanctions on their wealth abroad is a nightmare that they never anticipated. Their wealth is been reduced to nothingness and their life style badly affected. If they lean towards Putin the US and EU will squeeze harder, if they lean towards the West, Mr. Putin will pull the trigger at them. The question then is how long can the Oligarchs bear the consequences of Putin's war on their personal wealth at home and abroad. The primary objective of the sanctions is to squeeze Russia's wealthiest citizens to pressurize and compel them to put pressure on Putin to end his war in Ukraine. Then the other question is: can these people find any space to restrain Putin now that Putin has reduced their power and

The Oligarchs emerged in Russia with the emergence of the new Russia after the disintegration of the Soviet Union. The opportunities created by Russia's economic transition and privatization saw their emergence as Russia's elite money-bags and inner circle government brokers and influencers. But unknown to them, mean and calculating Vladamir Putin was not too comfortable with their expanding influence and when he strucked with the arrest and conviction of Mikhail Khodorkovsky, the wealhiest of the Olligarchs in 2003 the game changed, a perfect strike and the Oligarchs were caged. Gradually their influenced waned and their freedom and wealth were at the mercy of Mr.Putin . In other to reduce the effect of Putin's powers on their wealth they started investing off shore. The move was a smart one, but for the war in Ukraine. Now the intensity and dragnet of the US, EU and NATO sanctions on their wealth abroad is a nightmare that they never anticipated. Their wealth is been reduced to nothingness and their life style badly affected. If they lean towards Putin the US and EU will squeeze harder, if they lean towards the West, Mr. Putin will pull the trigger at them. The question then is how long can the Oligarchs bear the consequences of Putin's war on their personal wealth at home and abroad. The primary objective of the sanctions is to squeeze Russia's wealthiest citizens to pressurize and compel them to put pressure on Putin to end his war in Ukraine. Then the other question is: can these people find any space to restrain Putin now that Putin has reduced their power and

influence to the bearest minimum. In retrospect, Putin himself had since created a new class of Oligarch, the SILOVARCHS whose wealth is dependent on Putin's patronage and in return they serve his needs especially in helping him consolidate power. As it is today, majority of the Oligarchs are in 'mute' mode and the only few who have commented on the war are doing so in whispers (many of them privileged to be living and own businesses abroad). To buttress Putin's God like image in Russia, one analyst described a scene that played out on February 21 in a Security Council Meeting before the invasion of Ukraine.

The analyst cited that Sergey Naryshkam, director of Russia's Foreign Intelligence Service stammered when Putin asked if he supported recognizing the independence of Donesk and Luhansk. According to the analyst the way Putin spoke to him made him so scared, that he forgot what topic was being discussed.

To put it mildly, all Russians; the ordinary people, the Oligarchs and Silovarchs, the military and the government officials are all under Putin's spell and no one want to be a victim of his absolute power. Only time will tell whether the people of Russia can galvanize to play the "Russian Roullete" for Mr. Putin.

"For twenty years of my diplomatic career I have seen different turns of our foreign policy, but never have I been so ashamed of my country as on February 24 2022"

"Those who conceived this war want only one thing; to remain in power forever, live in pompous tasteless palaces, sail on yatchs comparable in tonnage and cost to the entire Russian navy, enjoying unlimited power and complete impunity, and to achieve this, they are willing to sacrifice as many lives as it takes. Thousands of Russians and Ukrainians have already died just for this"

- Boris Bondarev, counselor of the Permanent Mission of the Russian Federation to the United Nations.

DEMYSTIFYING RUSSIA'S MILITARY MYTH.

Russia puts a lot of love and money into its military. Russia is not new to wars neither does she shy away from wars. Russia is ever ready to give blood and much more ready to suck more blood than it gives. It is no pretence that Alina Kabaeva, a supposed girl friend of Putin, in a public event to boost support for Putin's war, said that wars are the heritage of Russia. "we inherited wars" said she and likened the Ukraine invasion to victory over World War ii Nazi. Indeed, Russia inherited wars; Russia has tested war destructions and tested much more war conquests. From Peter De Great to Vladamir Lenin to Joseph Stalin, Russia had raised one of the most formidable armies in human history (THE RED ARMY). Perhaps, Russia's respect in the international community comes from the feat of it's armies over the years. The Russian army is revered and respected and any leader that unmasked that myth will have to contend with another sword of democles.

The invasion of Ukraine by Putin was meant to be a swift and decisive victory with Ukrainians 'throwing flowers and kisses' at Mr. Putin shouting "Hosana … Hosana.. ! praise be unto Putin the liberator of Ukraine' but he was confounded with Ukraine resistance and loyalty to their sovereignty. He could not get Zelensky, he could not over-run kiev, then he changed tactics to bomb out the southern and eastern axis of Ukraine.

If Putin fails in the Ukraine invasion, the people of Russia will see it as a let down to their revered army, and the seed of resentment which has already been sewn, that the war is not Russias war, but Putin's personal war will be enough reason for the people of Russia to demand for his head.

A psychic in Russia by name, Alexander Kontonistov has in many occassions through his predictions spoken the mind of the average Russian on this. Once he projected that life would become harsher for the general population of Russia, which would lead to a growing dissatisfaction throughout the country. The psychic also claims that "the height of his life" (Putin) delivers the highest "chance of his death " which means that the dictator may kaput in the course of his war via his numerous sword of democles.

RUSSIA'S WARS

From the last century to date Russia has tested wars and war victories:

1924: the August uprising involving Russia (Soviet Union) and Danikom- victorious Russia

1925 – 1926: the Urtatagai conflict involving Soviet Union and the emirates of Afghanistan-

victorious Russia

1929 : Sino – Soviet war involving Soviet Union and China- victorious Russia

1932: Chechen uprising involving the Soviet Union and Chechen rebels- victorious Russia

1932 – 1941: Soviet -Japanese border conflict involving the Soviet union, Japan and Mongolia-settlement.

1914-1918: World War I involving the Allied Powers and the Central Powers with Russia fighting on the side of the victorious Allied Forces

1939 – 1945: wars of the World War II involving the Allied powers and the Axis powers of which Russia's Soviet union fought on the side of the victorious Allied Powers.

**Peter De Great

Born June 1672 in Moscow and died February 8 1728 in St. Petersburg . He was the Czar until 1721 when he proclaimed himself an emperor after expanding Russia into an empire and a major European power. His rule was characterized by military, political, economic and cultural reforms based on western European models. He was one of Russia's greatest statesmen. He founded the city of St. Petersburg and the erstwhile Romanov Dynasty.

**Vladimir Lenin

Born 12 April 1870 as Vladamir Ulynov and died January 1924. Vladamir Lenin was the leader of the revolution that brought down the Romavov dynasty that have ruled Russia since the time of Peter the great. He served as the first and founding head of government of Russia and later the

Soviet union from 1917 to 1924. Under his leadership the Soviet union became a one party socialist state governed by the Communist Party.

****Joseph Stalin**

 Born 1878. From 1928 until his death in 1953, Joseph Stalin ruled the Soviet Union as a dictator, transforming the country from an agrarian peasant society into a global superpower, though with a huge cost: Stalin was responsible for the deaths of millions of Soviet citizens. However, Soviet Union under his leadership was critical to the victory of the Allied Forces over Germany and the Axis Powers.

"NATIONS ARE ADVANCING AND AMASSING WEAPONS OF MASS DESTRUCTION TO 'DERER WAR' BUT IN REAL TERMS THEY ARE PREPARING FOR ARMAGEDDON "

- REUBEN-LAURENCE NZEWI

CHAPTER 10

THE INNOCENT CASUALTIES.

I read this profound testament in the social media.

Excerpt:

"For quite sometime now, I have relinquished the viewing right of the television set in my living room to my kids…. It was a deal, a kind of gentleman agreement … either I install another set in their bedroom or I relinquish the viewing right of the set in the living room to them which I agreed to. This means that I have to wait until they are tired or retired before I can view. But there is a clause that allows me to take permission from them if I want to interrupt their viewing …. So on a particular day I came back from my office and wanted to catch up with the headlines, so I sought permission and it was granted. I was given '10minutes' only. So I switched channels and it was Putin's Russia as usual and his bombardment of Ukraine. And the news highlights was on the war crimes the Russian soldiers are committing; Lots of violence and macabre scenes. My eyes were glued to the screen, so were my children's as the scenes were unfolding. So they took in everything and the questions started…. "Daddy, Daddy will Russia come to our house to kill all of us" ; that was my 8 years old daughter with panick in her eyes.

"Daddy, Daddy is Russia a devil ?....I hate Russia, they are killing every body" ; that was my 7 years old son.

"Daddy, I don't like Russia, I will tell my teacher" , said my 3 year old son.

53

There have been torrents of questions since then and sometime they feel I'm not answering their question well, so they decided to be asking their 'oracle' Google. Of course I'm the one that told them that Google knows everything as a way of letting them know that smart phones are not just for cartoon and music, and Google has not disappointed them either. All the questions they have asked Google, Google has answered so well. So they have come to trust Google. So whenever Daddy can not answer their questions they go to Google. On another day, it was a Sunday, my seven year old son asked me 'Daddy can I borrow your phone" and I replied "for what?" And he said "I want to ask Google something", so I obliged him. He and his siblings sat on the floor, three of them, as they glued their eyes to the phone screen. Now they called out "Daddy, Daddy come and see". They passed the phone over to me and this is what I saw on the scene UKRAINE WAR: "Putin Satan in human form" then my 8 years old daughter exclaimed "I know it, Putin is Satan, that is why he is killing everybody; that is what our teacher told us that Satan kill people, and my son asked spontaneously "So Daddy Satan is handsome (referring to Putin in his usual immaculate suit) before my 3 years old son interjected "Satan is not my friend, only Jesus that I like".

After reading this excerpt, I now understand Zelensky's prayers that God should restore the 'happiness of children'. I believe this kind of conversation is going on in many homes around the world, which tells us what Ukrainian children are going through in the face of the crisis. Ofcourse, Russian childrens too, as they are exposed to the vulgarity of the war. Indeed, Putin has murdered the innocence of children with his war.

"LET'S GIVE LOVE SO THAT IT SHALL BE RETURNED TO US"

-REUBEN-LAURENCE NZEWI

CHAPTER 11

THE FOOLS GAME

Now that the chicken have come home to roost; you deter me, I deter you, is the fools game. No man lives under the notion that the neighbor next door has the means to quench his life without doing something to neutralize and counter such threat. And this is the genesis of deadly weapon proliferation.

 It is usual for kids to be attracted to fire: cooking fire, candle fire, lamp fire and any other kind of fire provided it has a red glow. And parents normally have hard time trying to shout to kids to stay away from fire..., but when parents are tired of shouting, they may decide to ignore the child, maybe for a split second to get a taste of the fire to understand first hand that fire is not a toy; my mum did that to me and my siblings as a deterrent.

Just like parents, the holy spirit has been trying to persuade mankind to stay away from deadly weapons of mass destruction but humanity have been adamant Mankind is eager to have a taste of a nuclear weapon, notwithstanding that it saw what the atomic bomb did, when the US detonated the 'little boy' in Hiroshima and the 'fat man' in Nagasaki in1945 – even the atomic bomb is primitive compared to nuclear bomb. Perhaps the holy spirit like parents may decide to take his eyes off mankind so that humanity can get a taste of the nuclear bomb before understanding that it is not a toy.

" I know not what weapon will be used to fight the third world war, but I know the fourth world war will be fought with sticks and stones "

- Albert Einstein

What Einstein is saying in essence is that after the third world war, there will be nothing left of this civilization. Incase you don't know. Einstein is one of the brains behind the atomic bomb and advancement of the nuclear bomb. So he was just sounding a warning that humanity should stay away from nuclear armament.

If leaders around the world do not commit themselves to renewed cooperation in the many ways and avenues available for reducing existencial risks. And citizens of the world organizing themselves to demand that their leaders do so, the people of the world should be prepared to pay the 'debt of deceit'.

"If you stop, I stop.....who stops first":

If the US does not stop advancing and amassing nuclear weapons, Russia will not stop, if Russia does not stop, North- Korea will not stop, neither will Iran stop and nobody has the moral right to ask anybody to stop. So who is fooling who?

THE DOOMSDAY CLOCK

Incase you have not heard of it, the doomsday clock is an apocalyptic clock created by former Manhattan Project Scientists (makers of the first atomic bomb) in an effort to bring public attention to the threat of nuclear war. The doomsday clock is a symbol that represents the likelihood of a man-made global catastrophe. The clock depicts how close humanity is to armageddon and hovers anywhere between 17 and 2 minutes to midnight since it's formation.

The minute hand of the clock advances forward according to the threat level of a nuclear catastrophe. And since the Russia invasion of Ukraine, the clock has made a move closer to midnight in reaction to Putin's threat of nuclear attack.

* Is this the Ukrainian sovereignty "question" ?

* Is this Vladamir Putin's final "solution" ?

* Is this the World war III ?

* Will Vladamir Putin push the doomsday clock to hit midnight ?